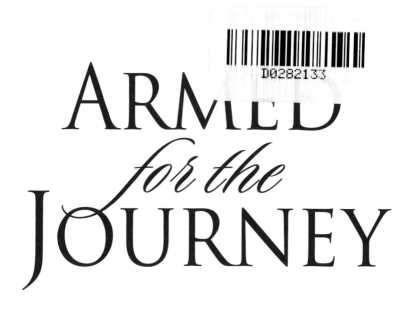

ARMED
for the
JOURNEY

MERCIDIEU
PHILLIPS

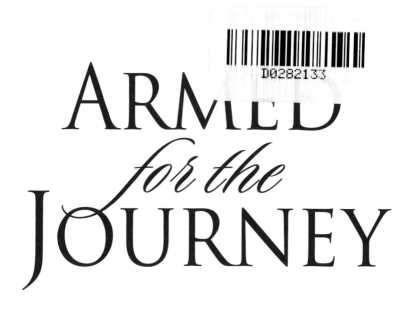

CREATION
HOUSE

ARMED FOR THE JOURNEY by Mercidieu Phillips
Published by Creation House
A Strang Company
600 Rinehart Road
Lake Mary, Florida 32746
www.creationhouse.com

Unless otherwise marked Scripture quotations are from the New American Standard Bible. Copyright © 1960, 1962, 1963, 1968, 1971, 1972, 1973, 1975, 1977 by the Lockman Foundation. Used by permission. (www.Lockman.org)

Scripture quotations marked NIV are from the Holy Bible, New International Version. Copyright © 1973, 1978, 1984, International Bible Society. Used by permission.

Cover design by Bill Johnson

Library of Congress Control Number 2007929196
International Standard Book Number 978-1-59979-236-1

First Edition

07 08 09 10 11 — 9 8 7 6 5 4 3 2 1
Printed in the United States of America

To my family: Emma, Jehiel, and Hadassah

You are God's priceless gift to me.

ACKNOWLEDGMENTS

A S I SURVEY the landscape of the church, I have been reflecting, thinking, and struggling with the condition of individuals, families, and society as a whole. These unanswered feelings drove me to commit to a greater understanding of the great divide between what God has promised us and what is actually happening.

This book is a result of the partial answers I have gleaned from biblical truths contained in God's infallible word. Thank You, Holy Spirit, for guiding me on this journey towards a beginner's understanding of spiritual matters and how they affect our daily lives. Thank you to Wesley Rose, my dear brother (mentor), and his wife, Anatine, who believed in me when that was a solo risk! Thank you, Agape Christian Fellowship, for your kindness and love in allowing me to pastor you with great joy and fulfillment. You are the best church family. Special thanks to the dedicated staff, leaders, and pastors (Louis Honorè and Barney Valcin), and my great administrative assistant, Odile Plancher. Special thanks to my dear friend and intercessor. Your prayers and unwavering support have been a constant source of encouragement. Thank you to two faithful servant leaders (Miriam and Lionel). A heartfelt thank you to House of the

Living God (Mirielle Simon), Shalom Community Church (Joanem Floral), Tabernacle of Glory (Gregory Toussaint), and Shiloh Ministries (Andre Laurent). Thanks also to my faithful ministry friends and partners worldwide. There are too many of you to mention here by name.

Special thanks also to Steve Smith and Steve Johnson for your unwavering trust and belief in me as an emerging leader. I am forever indebted also to the knees of so many caring people and ministry supporters. My "Thursday morning" crew, thanks for your prayers and support. Thanks also to the Strang Communications family. You have given me the reality of a cherished dream.

Finally, I am grateful to God's grace and favor in granting me the privilege to read and understand His Holy word.

CONTENTS

FOREWORD

A S SHE BOARDED the congested jet leaving from Haiti, the assurance of a better life engulfed her senses. My mother-in-law was so sure that this was the beginning of a new chapter in her life that she could see, hear, smell, taste, and even touch prosperity. Upon her arrival onto the soil of New York City in the late 1970's, she was suddenly hauled back into reality. Not having her legal papers, she had to work odd jobs to make a living. The certainty of a prosperous life was no longer present.

Ten years later when my mother-in-law started making arrangements to get her Green Card in order to go to school and get a substantive job, the news dropped on her like a ton of bricks—she had been granted an immediate Green Card the moment she touched ground in the United States based on her last name. Yes! She worked ten years as an illegal alien without an education while her Green Card lay dormant in someone's desk drawer collecting dust. The same is true for Christians today.

Unaware of the authority that they possess in Christ, the children of God much too often allow themselves to be oppressed by Satan whose sole purpose is to steal, kill, and destroy. (See John. 10:10.) In Hosea 4:16 the Bible teaches that God's people perish from lack of knowledge. Often when Christians are confronted with life's many challenges, they tend to buckle under pressure rather than tap into God's provisions for their lives.

I am so thrilled that God has raised up voices among us to remind His children of the authority that we possess through Christ Jesus. My dear spiritual brother and friend, Mercidieu Phillips, is an anointed servant who has answered such a call. Armed for the Journey challenges the children of God to stand up for their provisions in Jesus Christ. We are not looking to be blessed—we are blessed! Thank God for Mercidieu Phillips and his gift of revelation. I guarantee you will find this book to be a sword in your hand to slice through the deception of the enemy.

—GREGORY TOUSSAINT, B.S; Th.M; D.E.A.
Pastor, Tabernacle of Glory, Miami, Florida
Founder, GEM Ministries
http://www.gregorytoussaint.com

INTRODUCTION

And having disarmed the powers and authorities,
he made a public spectacle of them,
triumphing over them by the cross.

—COLOSSIANS 2:15, NIV

ONE OF THE greatest deficits that occur in the Christian life is the lack of understanding concerning the God-given authority each believer is granted upon acceptance of the Lord Jesus Christ. If you take a closer look at your Bible, you find that the idea of spiritual authority permeates Scripture from Genesis to Revelation. The story of creation is a manifestation of God's divine authority and power. The first and second chapters of Genesis declare that God "spoke" everything into existence. He could have easily mobilized an army of angels to embark on an extensive construction project, but instead He decided to demonstrate His unquestioned authority over nature and speak order on an earth that was dark and void. There is no greater demonstration of sovereignty.

The very first recorded verbal communication God had with His crown jewel, Adam was an announcement of responsibility and authority. The texts reads, "God blessed them and said to them, 'Be fruitful and increase in number; fill the earth and subdue it. Rule over the fish of the sea and the birds of the air and over every living creature that moves on the ground'" (Gen. 1:28, NIV). God gave Adam dominion over the things that He created. In other words, when God breathed His breath into Adam, at that moment Adam possessed divine authority, however God had to announce it to him for him to begin using it. Through His written Word, God has announced and continues to announce that you and I also have that same authority. Understanding and living in that timeless reality is indeed a powerful thing to embrace!

The introduction of sin by Satan coupled with Adam and Eve's unexplainable submission to the tempter, temporarily stripped man of this authority. Satan being the crafty individual knew that in order to effectively wage war against God, he would have to do so by diminishing the authority of man. Indeed, he temporarily succeeded by successfully breaking man's relationship with his Creator. Nevertheless, God provided a redemptive plan to equip man with what he lost. Consequently, it took the redemptive work of Christ to restore it in our lives again. However, the enemy does not want you to live in the restored nature granted by the work of Christ. He would much rather see you live a life of continual defeat and despair. As a true believer in the resurrected Christ, I want to remind you that you have four principle enemies. They are self (you), the world, the flesh, and Satan. Each of these domains represents a constant exchange between the spirits patrolling the air and the Spirit of God. These four enemies also stand as the fundamental reason we seek to embody the authority declared in our favor. While God has graciously given us victory over them there is no assurance that they are eliminated with that knowledge alone. The ever-reaching grip of sin has undoubtedly proven for the time you are granted life on this earth, you will have to deal with each of them at certain moments and intersections of your life. As I share with you some insight on spiritual warfare, God has led me to do it on the side of victory. You are already victorious because Satan is a defeated adversary who will never equal the power and authority of Jesus.

The theological approach and scriptural references represents the profound conviction that I personally possess and hope to expose you to. Your time in this work will prove these are vital and relevant for today as you attempt to gain a greater awareness of your position and that of the enemy. The church though growing in numbers have been reduced to spiritual impotence due to the silence or rather selective indifference to the reality of spiritual warfare. I argue in this book that God did not intend for His children to live a defeated life, but to know victory in every area.

Further, I argue that as believers we possess more authority than we think. Therefore, we must move with boldness to activate what God has already declared ours! There is no doubt that the pervasiveness of sin and escalating global scale of evil has created a valid question that must be addressed. The collective chaos and destruction we experience as a society curiously interrogates the existence of the church as the body of Christ. Where has the power and authority described in the Gospel of Mark 16:17–18 gone?

Furthermore, we are forced to ask is the world getting darker or has the light diminished to a barely lit flickering flame?

My motivation and purpose for writing this book is to help you understand and reclaim the authority that you have been given as a child of God. As you read this work, I hope it will leave you with two major impressions. First, I hope you begin to understand your rightful position as a child of God. Jesus declared us to be His when he paid the price for our past, present and future transgressions at Calvary. My goal is to get you to accept without a doubt that you belong to the living God. He is your Father and therefore He has vested you with authority and rights over the enemy. The truth contained in Scripture and noted in this work presents an abundance of evidence to that end. Second, it is my earnest prayer that your life will begin to experience a catalytic revolution that will usher you into your destiny.

Principle 1

UNDERSTANDING THE ENEMY

Be self-controlled and alert. Your enemy the devil prowls around like a roaring lion looking for someone to devour.

—1 Peter 5:8, niv

IF YOU HAVE ever watched the discovery channel, you have no doubt seen images of a lion. The lion is considered as the most dangerous animal of the jungle. It posses an incredible amount of strength and can move faster than you can run. He uses a method of intimidation to conquer its prey. The roar of his voice paralyzes its prey, thus, lessening his efforts to hunt them down.

Andre was just leaving church after a powerful time in the presence of God. He had just heard a powerful sermon on fear. The speaker's eloquence and forceful delivery stirred in Andre a feeling of conqueror. He left church singing and overflowing with the joy of the Spirit. There was one problem; a young man who was also at the service decided to play a prank on Andre. The young man left moments before the closing prayer and hid himself behind a series of trees along the route Andre would be taking back home. Upon hearing Andre's footstep and hearing his voice singing about victory, the young man jumped out of the bush with the roar of a lion. Andre was shaken to the point he forgot everything he had just claimed as a child of God. The young man pretended to be a foe and Andre began negotiating with a make-believe force.

Peter's description of Satan as a lion is on point. We know that he is powerful, deceptive, and moves very swiftly if given the opportunity. He roars in our lives with issues that often cause us to tremble in fear and worry. You need to know that, He is not out to just scare or irritate you, but he is out for total destruction. His highest goal is to completely destroy us.

There is one major reason for this relentless pursuit. Man is created in the image of God. Furthermore, the psalmist notes that man has been "crowned with glory and majesty" (Ps. 8:5, author's paraphrase). Let that simmer in your mind for a while. God has shared one of His attributes with man. Satan on the other hand hates anything that glorifies God. Because man's ultimate purpose is to glorify God and God has given him the means to do so, Satan will stop at nothing to forbid that from happening. Please understand that the intent of the enemy is to rip your heart out. The very thing that God desires and speaks of most in His Word is the one thing the enemy is out to destroy. The enemy is tenacious in all his attempts and he is relentless in his pursuit of the child of God. Remember, you are the subject of an epic battle between Jehovah and Satan.

> Remember, you are the subject of an
> epic battle between Jehovah and Satan.

God created man to live in peace and to be a walking image of Him. For two and a half chapters of the creation story, we see that very intent on display. The fellowship between God and man was uninterrupted for a period of time unknown to any scholar. However, from the beginning to the third chapter to this very minute of your reading, the battle has been raging. How did we become engaged? God is the sole Keeper of that mystery!

I would be negligent in my responsibility not to remind you that Christianity is not the movement it has been portrayed to be by those who are on your plasma television or on the cover of the latest self help book or compact disc. It is a far cry from the therapeutic gospel of our day that encourages people further in their self-centered pursuit of God's provisions. Moreover, it is not the movement that removes every sense of obligation and vigilance to sin. Christianity at its very core is a war. The forces of darkness are against the Son of God and all those who claim Him as Lord and Savior. We have to live everyday with the thought that Satan does not like us and is out to prove that with every opportunity given.

On the other hand, you have to know that even though he is a lion, he is a defeated lion. A lion that has no bite because his teeth were crushed at the same time his head was crushed. (See Genesis 3:15.) The roaring of the lion is only heard when we either intentionally or unintentionally quiet the voice of our savior through the abandonment of spiritual disciplines such as prayer, fasting, meditation of the Word, and continual worship. The intention of the enemy is to overpower what he knows is in you with fear and intimidation.

> The roaring of the lion is only heard when we either intentionally or unintentionally quiet the voice of our savior through the abandonment of spiritual disciplines such as prayer, fasting, meditation of the Word, and continual worship.

As you are reading this you may be going through a series of events in your life that has you worried beyond reason. My friend, please remember that worry is one of the preferred weapons of the enemy. Understanding the destructive potential of worry, Jesus addresses this as He wisely exhorts, "Do not be anxious for tomorrow; for tomorrow will care for itself," and adds, "Which of you by being anxious can add a single cubit to his life's span?" (Matt. 6:34, 27 respectively). Indeed, the unannounced attacks of the enemy may seem to be fast and consistent. The faith you have demonstrated in the past is weakening with each fury. I want to challenge you to commit once again to your task at hand. Faith rises in proportion to revelation. With revelation comes responsibility. God has helped you understand that your enemy is a lion, a defeated lion that is seeking to devour you. You are halfway to victory in knowing the nature of the enemy.

Begin your new walk today by confessing that you are not afraid of a defeated lion.

ACTION ITEMS

1. Recognize that you are in warfare:
   - *Biblical truth* "For our struggle is not against flesh and blood, but against the rulers, against the powers, against the world forces of this darkness, against the spiritual forces of wickedness in the heavenly places" (Eph. 6:12).

2. Learn the tactics of the enemy:
   - *Biblical truth* "And no wonder, for even Satan disguises himself as an angel of light. Therefore it is not surprising if his servants also disguise themselves as servants of righteousness; whose end shall be according to their deeds" (2 Cor. 11:14–15).

3. Do not be deceived:
   - *Biblical truth* "See to it that no one takes you captive through philosophy and empty deception, according to the tradition of men, according to the elementary principles of the world, rather than according to Christ" (Col. 2:8).

STEPS FOR TODAY

1. Ask yourself the why question each time before making a decision.

2. Practice self-talk by repeating this verse when you begin feeling overwhelmed.

STUDY QUESTIONS

1. What signs of spiritual warfare have you noticed in your life lately?

2. From your earliest memory, what image of Satan have you been accustomed to seeing or hearing?

3. Are there any positive images of a lion in the Bible?

Principle 2

UNMASKING THE ENEMY

The thief comes only to steal and kill and destroy;
I have come that they may have life,
and have it to the full.

—JOHN 10:10, NIV

M OST PROFESSIONAL SPORTS teams spend a great amount of money on scouts. Their job is to go and investigate the tendencies and tactics of the opposing teams. These scouts have a responsibility to come back and report their findings to their respective teams. The game plan and victory of the team rests heavily on their due diligence. Through His never-changing Word God has given us the scouting report on this adversary. The report is accurate and intimidating minus the provision of Christ. Regrettably, our churches have shifted the focus off the truth about this adversary and have numbed the conscience of its people to an impalpable status. Hence, though more people are seeking religion and spirituality, the mounting deficit in knowledge and awareness continues to be at an all-time high. For example, Satan is usually depicted as an individual with two horns wielding a pitchfork. These images stamp the feeble mind of those who are ignorant to the real description of him. Some of the ways Scripture depicts him for us is as a thief, the father of lies, a deceiver, the tempter, and as Satan. Let's take a closer look at each of these descriptions.

Thief

The Bible says that as a thief he comes to steal, kill, and destroy. The plan of the enemy is to constantly steal your joy, happiness, peace and hope. His fiery darts aims directly for our inner emotions. Have you been around a Christian who is just never happy? Their entire life is spent whining and complaining about how hard life is. Chances are this person has been a victim of this serial thief. Not only does he come to steal, but he also seeks to kill. One of the first things he attempts to kill is your motivation. Have you ever wondered why so many people give up on their dreams, careers, callings, or relationships? The answer lies in the truth of "murdered motivation"—once you lose your motivation, all your actions will yield a negative return because you are merely functioning, but with no real expectations. The enemy has effectively used this weapon in families, marriages, and even in the church. People are just not willing to give what is important a second chance. They quit at the first sign of trouble! Why? The assassin had successfully killed their drive. Additionally, he comes to destroy our physical and emotional health. For some he rages warfare with known and unknown diseases and illnesses. For others, he attacks their mind with waves of discouragement and depression ultimately leading to ongoing thoughts of suicide. Let me assure you that he cannot do any of these things to you because you are covered by the blood of Jesus!

Father of Lies

The students of biology will quickly agree with me when I say that life comes from the father via the blood. When the Bible describes the enemy as the father of lies, God is actually announcing to us that the life of deception and falsehoods are rooted firmly in the characteristic of Satan. Remember how he lied about the purpose and vision of God to Adam and Eve in the Garden of Eden? He still continues to do this today. Often he will whisper in your ear that God has forgotten you and you are simply wasting your time in this whole faith business. Moreover, he will make things and issues seem bigger than they are for the sake of bringing fear into your life. He lies to our children through false teaching at school and in college courses. Today his greatest tools are culture and religion. To know and understand when you are being lied to, you must know the truth. This truth is discovered in the Word of God and through a persistent life of consecration.

Deceiver

Because the enemy is the father of all lies, he uses deception as a major tool to fight the children of God. There is no greater time of deception than the hour in which we live. Jesus announced this in His Olivet discourse when he said, "Watch out that no one deceives you. For many will come in my name, claiming, 'I am the Christ,' and will deceive many" (Matt. 24:4–5, NIV). His primary job is to present himself for what he is not. In order to distinguish him from our true Lord and Savior, you must become familiar with Jesus. Later, I will explain some specific steps for you to do this.

Tempter

One of the greatest truths I discovered in Scripture is the fact that the enemy has no power to make the believer do anything. His strategic schemes are limited in nature. He only has the ability to tempt you to obey his wishes. Remember the scene with Jesus on the temple overlooking Jerusalem. He had an opportunity to push Christ. However, he asked Christ to push himself down and allow the angels to come and rescue him. What a coward! He can only provide the opportunity to you, but the decision is entirely up to you. What is your decision?

ACTION ITEMS

1. Guard your mind:
    - *Biblical truth* "And the peace of God, which surpasses all comprehension, shall guard your hearts and your minds in Christ Jesus" (Phil. 4:7).

2. Intentionally submit to God:

- *Biblical truth* "Submit yourselves, then, to God. Resist the devil, and he will flee from you" (James 4:7, NIV).

3. Acknowledge the existence of weapons:
   - *Biblical truth* "'No weapon that is formed against you shall prosper; and every tongue that accuses you in judgment you will condemn. This is the heritage of the servants of the LORD, and their vindication is from Me,' declares the LORD" (Isa. 54:17).

STEPS FOR TODAY

1. Promise not to participate in any type of ungodly storytelling (gossip).

2. Spend the day praying in two-minute intervals.

STUDY QUESTIONS

1. What new insights do you have about the enemy?

2. Can you identify some spiritual of the weapons you think the enemy has tried to use against you lately?

3. How do you plan to overcome the tactics of Satan?

4. What feelings do you have knowing you have such an enemy?

Principle 3

THE SOURCE OF AUTHORITY

'I have given you authority to trample on snakes and scorpions and to overcome all the power of the enemy.

—LUKE 10:19, NIV

THE JOY OF this warfare is in knowing that you do not have to fight it in your own power. There has been a provision made for each child of God through the shed blood of Jesus. When Satan deceived Adam and Eve in the garden, he not only robbed them of their intimacy and fellowship with God, but he stripped them of the authority they possessed. The result of this is what we often refer to as the fallen nature that is unable to fight the enemy on its own. To understand this you only have to turn on the local news or pick up the morning paper. There you see and read about the struggle man faces to overcome the enemy on his own. People enter rehabs and many faith-based programs. Others faithfully attend anger management classes and great counseling programs. Their efforts, though noble in intent, fall short because they are unable to overcome the evil one with their own power.

Immediately after the Fall, God gave a clear indication of His intention to restore that power again in man. He announced these words, also known as the first messianic prophecy, "And I will put enmity between...your offspring and hers; he will crush your head, and you will strike his heel" (Gen. 3:15, NIV). Those powerful, prophetic words paved the way for the ultimate defeat exhibited at Calvary. When Jesus willingly died on the cross, and rose from the dead, He essentially gave birth to the power of God that is available to every believer. As a believer you need to live with the assurance that Satan is a defeated foe. He knows that, but is willing to take a chance to get you to believe that he is in control. Jesus has defeated Satan and manifests that defeat each time you are delivered from an attack! For this reason, we know that there are three things that the enemy would rather not hear. I am going to list them for you and expound on each in a detailed manner for your understanding.

> Jesus has defeated Satan and manifests that defeat each time you are delivered from an attack!

THE NAME OF JESUS

Names are significant in that they help us remember the action and influence of particular individuals. There are names that are synonymous with certain undeniable moments in the course of human history. The name Adolph

Hitler is a vivid reminder of the cruelty of the human heart towards its fellow man. Who can ever forget the tragedies we witnessed in Bosnia at the beginning of the nineties. The name Saddam Hussein carries with it, images of a strong leader whose personal ambitions drove him to a skewed sense of nationalism. On the other hand, there are other names that exude a warm sense of life. The name of Mother Theresa will always be linked to the level of personal sacrifice one can show in the name of God. The name of Dr. Martin Luther King Jr. is etched in American history for the courage he displayed in the face of evil. The Reverend Billy Graham will forever be remembered as the ultimate evangelist of America.

The name of Jesus is the greatest name! The name of Jesus is the believer's password to the throne room of heaven. We don't simply add it as garnish to the end of our elaborate prayers, but we call on that name because it is our key to the heart of the Father. In one of the most profound Christological passages in Scripture, the apostle Paul highlights the supremacy of that name:

> We don't simply add it as garnish to the end of our elaborate prayers, but we call on that name because it is our key to the heart of the Father.

Therefore God exalted him to the highest place and gave him the name that is above every name, that at the name of Jesus every knee should bow, in heaven and on earth and under the earth, and

> every tongue confess that Jesus Christ is Lord, to
> the glory of God the Father.
>
> —Philippians 2:9–11, NIV

At the beginning of the early church, Christians as well as non-Christians witnessed the power of that name. In Acts we read the account of a beggar who was accustomed to coming to the temple to ask for alms. However, this day would prove to be this man's last day of being in that position. After hearing this man's plea for another contribution, Peter and John fixed their eyes on the man and Peter said to him, "Look at us." When the man had given them his attention, Peter said, "The silver or gold I do not have, but what I have I give you. In the name of Jesus Christ of Nazareth, walk" (Acts 3:4–6, NIV). Immediately, Peter and John took the man up by the right hand and he experienced instant physical transformation for the very first time. Where the name of Jesus is mentioned there is power.

Jesus declared in John 16:23–24 that whatever you ask in His name, He will do it. That is power in its fullest form. As believers we have the ability to call on one name and receive answers for all our needs and troubles. The name of Jesus reminds Satan of how powerless he really is. At the name of Jesus, knees bow, demons tremble, fear flees and demonic forces are left to run into swines. The name of Jesus brings order where the adversary desires disorder! The enemy understands this and tries to keep you focused on your name or the name of your friends, family, teachers and sometimes enemies. Why? Because he knows the day you understand the power of the name of Jesus, you will begin to use it as your password to overcome him and his schemes. Make a commitment to begin using that name as the ultimate source of authority in you life.

> The name of Jesus brings order where the adversary desires disorder!

THE BLOOD OF JESUS

Our access to God is only through the shed blood of Jesus. His finished work on Calvary guarantees our rightful position as children of God. In the same manner God demonstrated man's inability to "cover" himself in the garden through the blood of Jesus, we receive the covering and forgiveness we need to stand before a holy God. The blood of Jesus removes the ugly stain left by sin. Throughout the Old Testament there are countless references to the process of sacrifice all of which included the shedding of animal blood. These acts were a foreshadowing of the ultimate shedding of blood, for John declared, "Behold, the Lamb of God who takes away the sin of the world!" (John 1:29). Under the old covenant the sins of the people were only "covered" for a year. Thus, they had to repeatedly go to the temple each year with a burnt offering to assure that they had "paid" their dues or spiritual taxes. Therefore, upon seeing Jesus, John was no doubt elated to finally find one person who would take care of this matter once and for all.

The blood of Jesus is a vivid reminder to Satan how he lost the battle for your soul. Each time that blood is mentioned, it's a slap in the face for the enemy. It is a bitter reminder to him that he has no authority over your life and your destiny. The blood of Jesus provides necessary protection from the vials and schemes of the evil one. It serves as a diffusing agent each time a missile is launched from the enemy's camp. When you pray in the name of Jesus, and in the power of His shed blood, you are putting the enemy on notice that you know your source.

> It serves as a diffusing agent each time a missile is launched from the enemy's camp.

CONFESSION OF THE WRITTEN WORD

In addition to the name of Jesus, the blood of Jesus, the enemy refuses to hear the written Word being quoted. Let me put it this way, the written Word is your ultimate source of live ammunition in your battle. God has provided specific missiles for specific attacks. The believer should understand the value of confessing the written Word. Jesus illustrated this for us during His personal encounter with the enemy. This encounter is detailed for us in this manner:

> The tempter came to him and said, "If you are the Son of God, tell these stones to become bread." Jesus answered, "It is written: 'Man does not live on bread alone, but on every word that comes from the mouth of God.'" Then the devil took him to the holy city and had him stand on the highest point of the temple. "If you are the Son of God," he said, "throw yourself down. For it is written: "'He

will command his angels concerning you, and they will lift you up in their hands, so that you will not strike your foot against a stone.'" Jesus answered him, "It is also written: 'Do not put the Lord your God to the test.'" Again, the devil took him to a very high mountain and showed him all the kingdoms of the world and their splendor. "All this I will give you," he said, "if you will bow down and worship me." Jesus said to him, "Away from me, Satan! For it is written: 'Worship the Lord your God, and serve him only.'"

—Matthew 4:3–10, NIV

The interesting thing in that entire passage is that Jesus spoke the written Word to the enemy to let him know the truth. This source of authority comes when you make yourself familiar with the Word of God. Having a tool and not using it is really silly. The work of resisting the enemy is not as difficult as we often make it seem. The truth of the matter is God's Word acts like a sword and shield to aid us in our march toward victory. There is no mention of Jesus using His own words to combat the enemy. He used what was already given to Him by the Father. I once heard a well-known speaker sum it up this way: if Jesus who is the living Word, needed the written Word to defeat the enemy of the Word, how much more should we use the Word? You can begin using this powerful tool today in your personal devotion and prayer time. The power to change your atmosphere is in your hand, on that coffee table, or even sitting on the shelf of your library. Becoming familiar with the Word is becoming familiar with victorious living.

> The truth of the matter is God's Word acts like a sword and shield to aid us in our march toward victory.

ACTION ITEMS

1. Commit to the Source:
   - *Biblical truth* "I am the vine, you are the branches; he who abides in Me, and I in him, he bears much fruit; for apart from Me you can do nothing" (John 15:5).

2. Trust the Source:
   - *Biblical truth* "Trust in the LORD with all your heart, and do not lean on your own understanding. In all your ways acknowledge Him, and He will make your paths straight" (Prov. 3:5–6).

3. Follow the Source:
   - *Biblical truth* "If anyone wishes to come after Me, let him deny himself, and take up his cross daily, and follow Me" (Luke 9:23).

STEPS FOR TODAY

1. Read 1 John 1:7 and meditate on that truth throughout your day.

2. Find songs that lift up the name of Jesus and sing about the name of Jesus today.

STUDY QUESTIONS

1. Have you ever had to bind the enemy and his demonic activity in a particular situation?

2. What insight has God given you about the source of your authority?

3. In what ways can you overcome the enemy in your personal battle?

Principle 4

THE USE OF AUTHORITY

Submit yourselves, then, to God.
Resist the devil, and he will flee from you.
Come near to God and he will come near to you.

—JAMES 4:7–8

T HE BATTLE THAT the believer fights is not fought on the basis of knowledge alone. Knowledge without application is reduced to information. Throughout this book, I have been outlining for you the different aspects of your authority and the enemy's nature. In this chapter I want to explore with you: (1) why it's important to use authority and, (2) how to use it effectively.

| Knowledge without application is
reduced to information.

In writing to the church at Ephesus, Paul noted that the battle is not against "flesh and blood" but against the forces of darkness. One truth that can be gleaned from this is that enemy is always willing to attack whenever he has opportunity to do so. I often say in my teachings, no matter the level of unemployment in any country, Satan is always employed. As long as there are genuine, sold out, committed followers of Jesus, Satan will always have work to do.

IT'S IMPORTANT

Iron sharpens iron! (See Proverbs 27:17.) If you are serious about enjoying a great piece of steak, you will no doubt have to use a steak knife. That does not mean you can't eat it without that particular tool, but it makes perfect sense to use one. You can agree with me that we are fighting an enemy who has authority. How do you fight with someone who is bigger than you? You will look for something that is bigger than you. Remember that before Goliath, David understood the power of that giant and all the armor he had with him. The words of David were key when he said, "You come to me with a sword, a spear, and a javelin, but I come in the name of the LORD of hosts, the God of the armies of Israel, whom you have taunted" (1 Sam. 17:45). That was a man using the authority that was available to him. It is important to use your divine authority because the enemy will not apologize for using his. He knows your limitations, but he doesn't know your ammunition.

> It is important to use your divine authority because the enemy will not apologize for using his.

During a heated NBA championship, the best-of-seven series was tied at three games apiece. When asked by a reporter what was his game plan, the star player for the underdog team, said, "If I am going down, I want to go down shooting the ball." We are not going down because Jesus took care of that already, however, if we are going to stand up, we must do so with the authority that has been given to us.

HOW TO EXERCISE AUTHORITY

Your responsibility it to make good use of the authority you have been given. There are three key principles that are necessary in your exercise of authority:

Prayer

When we truly decide to engage in a life of prayer, we are actually exercising dominion. Prayer has been defined by many as the believer's means of communicating with God. The fundamental truth of this limited definition is true; however such an incomplete version cannot bypass the crucial power of prayer as it relates to the spiritual realm. If we accept it as just communication of our needs to the supply warehouse of heaven, we have succeeded at trivializing the most important weapon needed to assure victory. A prominent theme throughout the ministry of Jesus is the necessity of prayer and was repeatedly illustrated by the Messiah Himself.

> If we accept it as just communication of our needs to the supply warehouse of heaven, we have succeeded at trivializing the most important weapon needed to assure victory.

Through prayer we see the awesome power of God coming alive on our personal lives. James captures this best when he writes, "The prayer of a righteous man is powerful and effective" (James 5:16, NIV). He goes on and uses Elijah as an example of how we can exercise our God-given authority through prayer. Jesus said that if you abide in Him and He in you, whatever you ask in His name shall be done. (See John 15:7.) Satan hates a praying Christian. Why? He knows that when the believer engages in prayer, he is tapping into a power source that he cannot dispute is more powerful than he and his kingdom. Hence, it is with the fear of a thief and the audacity of a vagabond that he attempts to interrupt our communion with God. He rests on this fundamental truth. If he can get you to minimize the power of prayer, he will get you to maximize your inability to overcome him. Jesus illustrated this authority for us in the Gospel of Matthew, "I will give you the keys of the kingdom of heaven; whatever you bind on earth will be bound in heaven, and whatever you loose on earth will be loosed in heaven" (Matt. 16:19, NIV).

Worship

More and more people are slowly discovering the power of worship in spiritual warfare. To worship is to acknowledge the essence of God. It is to proclaim and declare the sovereignty and the Holiness of Jehovah. Each time we decide to worship God, we remind the enemy of our affection for our Creator and our devotion to Him. Further, the intentional act of openly identifying with our risen Savior is a source of great remorse to the one whose former job was leading others in that same truth. No one wants to be constantly reminded of what they have lost. The greatest confusion you can place in the enemy's camp is to engage in worship when the circumstances around you say different. Remember Paul and Silas in that jail cell. Chained and badly beaten, they decided to exercise their authority by letting the enemy and the present circumstances know who was on the throne of their lives.

> The greatest confusion you can place in the enemy's camp is to engage in worship when the circumstances around you say different.

This account depicts the usage of authority through prayer and worship:

> After they had been severely flogged, they were thrown into prison, and the jailer was commanded to guard them carefully. Upon receiving such orders, he put them in the inner cell and fastened their feet in the stocks. About midnight Paul and Silas were praying and singing hymns to God, and the other prisoners were listening to them.

Suddenly there was such a violent earthquake that the foundations of the prison were shaken. At once all the prison doors flew open, and everybody's chains came loose.

—Acts 16:23–26, NIV

This is a powerful reminder about the response of God to a person who understands and uses their authority to fight the enemy. In your hands are all the necessary tools you need to overcome the adversary. The choice is yours to decide whether or not you will engage and experience victory.

ACTION ITEMS

1. Accept your position of authority:
   - *Biblical truth* "In all these things we are more than conquerors through him who loved us" (Rom. 8:37, NIV).

2. Live fearlessly:
   - *Biblical truth* "For God has not given us a spirit of timidity, but of power and love and discipline" (2 Tim. 1:7).

3. Rely on His presence:
   - *Biblical truth* "They looked to Him and were radiant, and their faces shall never be ashamed" (Ps. 34:5).

STEPS FOR TODAY

1. Confess the name of Jesus throughout the day.

2. Plead the blood of Jesus over your life and family.

STUDY QUESTIONS

1. Where do you look in times of crisis?

2. What is your perspective on authority in general?

3. What has God revealed to you about His abilities?

Principle 5

AUTHORITY OVER THE FAMILY

But as for me and my house, we will serve the LORD.
—JOSHUA 24:15

THE GREATEST THREAT facing our society today is the ongoing erosion of the family unit as originally intended by God. The constant resignation of the fathers from their divine responsibility creates an undesirable amount of single parent homes. This epidemic leads to children growing up without proper structures and guidelines necessary for the raising up of a mature adult. Before I continue with this, I must commend those mothers who have battled the odds to raise productive members of society. This is not an easy task and you ought to be commended for your acts of sheer heroism.

This problem is the direct result of a misunderstanding of the God-given authority that the man holds in the home. God told Adam that he was to "rule" and "dominate" over all that He had created. In addition to ruling over nature,

Adam was given the headship of the family unit. What a powerful responsibility! God had entrusted the progress of His most precious creation into the hand of Adam. Adam's divine responsibility was to provide leadership for his wife and the children they would later be granted. This pattern continued throughout Scripture as God always respected the role of the man when giving directives for a family, and even the nation.

There is no doubt that if the family unit is to become whole again, the divine authority and hierarchical structure of the home must return. Fathers can't lead away from home. Moreover, fathers will only lead in the direction they are headed. The Christian family must allow the Word of God to have its proper place in the affairs of the home. We gain authority in our families only when the authoritative Word is given its rightful place in our daily activities. Prayer must become a common practice and not just something the family does when there is a need for comfort. The family altar must be the place where everyone in the home meets with God. We have often heard the saying "a family that prays together, stays together". While this is not quoted in the Bible, the principle is clearly evident.

> We gain authority in our families only when the authoritative Word is given its rightful place in our daily activities.

By the authority vested in us, we must reclaim our families through an intentional return to the order established by God and clearly explained by the apostle Paul. He writes:

> Wives, submit to your husbands as to the Lord. For the husband is the head of the wife as Christ is the head of the church.…Husbands, love your wives, just as Christ loved the church and gave himself up for her.…and the wife must respect her husband.…Children, obey your parents in the Lord, for this is right. "Honor your father and mother".…Fathers, do not exasperate your children; instead, bring them up in the training and instruction of the Lord.
>
> —Ephesians 5:22–23, 25, 33; 6:1–2, 4, NIV

In the twenty-first century, the most challenging menace to society is not global warming, global unrest, or the threat of evil men destroying each other through acts of hatred and violence, but the greatest danger is the deterioration of the center of civilization, the family. No political party, agenda, or public policy can correct this problem. The solution is found only in the intentional application of God's Word. Jesus said you, "Shall know the truth, and the truth shall make you free" (John 8:32). Freedom is authority! Speak to someone who has been held against their will and now is free again. They will tell you that they feel some sense of control over their lives again. Why? Freedom is authority. The authority of the family is in knowing how God has designed the operation of that unit. When the family understands God's plan, the members are free to live in harmony with one another because the threat of suppression is no longer.

> The greatest danger is the deterioration of the center of civilization, the family.

The failure to gain authority over your family leads to a disconnect with self. You cannot become the person God has called you to be if you're not connected to your foundation. People can go on and be successful in their careers and ministries, but there is a division within the mind because visible success cannot replace inner voids.

> You cannot become the person God has called you to be if you're not connected to your foundation.

If a survey were taken the consensus would be that the lack of leadership from fathers has created an entire generation of young men who are at lost on how to lead families of their own. More than that, many of them don't even see the need to create a family. The statistics on the divorce and the impact on children are staggering. The broken image of marriage encourages this generation to fear and shun the idea of altogether. What happens? Well, you guessed it. More people are living promiscuous lives and some have ventured into a lifestyle that is being forcefully marketed as "alternative." The followers of Jesus Christ cannot afford to allow the ongoing degradation of the family unit. The victim of such colossal negligence is a society searching for answers. The price is greater than the national debt and we are left to file for moral bankruptcy. Can we afford to not take authority over our families? The answer is before our eyes as we witness school shootings and senseless acts of violence.

Yes, this is a voice crying in the wilderness for the re-establishment of the family. This will only happen when we understand that God has given us the authority to create and manage this complex, but sacred institution. Are you on your way to reclaiming that missing piece to your family? I hope so!

ACTION ITEMS

1. Cultivate a spirit of forgiveness:
   - *Biblical truth* "And be kind to one another, tender-hearted, forgiving each other, just as God in Christ also has forgiven you" (Eph. 4:32).

2. Create a family altar:
   - *Biblical truth* "The effective prayer of a righteous man can accomplish much" (James 5:16).

3. Follow His lead:
   - *Biblical truth* "Unless the LORD builds the house, they labor in vain who build it" (Ps. 127:1).

STEPS FOR TODAY

1. Do something for someone in your family who does not deserve it.

2. Pray for peace and unity in your family.

STUDY QUESTIONS

1. How are the spiritual needs of your family being met?

2. Are you praying for your family on a daily basis?

3. What role do you play in family conflicts?

Interlude

CLOSING OPEN DOORS

Set a guard, O LORD, over my mouth;
keep watch over the door of my lips.
Do not incline my heart to any evil thing,
to practice deeds of wickedness.

—PSALM 141:3–4

BEFORE WE CONTINUE our exploration of some additional principles to assist you in the battle against the enemy, it is paramount that I share with you the necessity of understanding how Satan often tries to enter a person, especially those who belong to Christ. Have you ever tried to understand how some people arrive at their current place of turmoil? Better yet, have you often sat and wondered where you picked up this thing you find yourself doing even against your desire? Unlike God who does not need your assistance to save you, the enemy needs every bit of your help for him to destroy you. Whoa! Are you serious

Phil? This is what I trust the following pages will help you understand.

In the beginning sections, I introduced you to the reality of the warfare believers are actively engaged in. Understanding that our fight is not against flesh and blood, but against the principalities and rulers of the air is crucial to living a victorious life in Christ Jesus. It is safe to say that understanding the existence of the enemy is not enough if one is ever going to win this battle.

Equally important to the knowledge of your enemy is understanding not only how he operates, but also how he enters into someone's life. The work of the cross rendered the enemy rendered ineffective by Jesus Christ. Nevertheless, his lack of power does not eliminate his passion or his deadly schemes. Because of his inability to control or possess the child of God, he often enters in a person's life with their cooperation. How is this possible you might ask? Well, his strategy is to get you to open doors that will facilitate his easy entry.

> Because of his inability to control or possess the child of God, he often enters in a person's life with their cooperation.

These doors are often things we think very little of. For instance, one of the ways Satan could enter a person is through the door of discouragement. Discouragement can grow like a cancer if not treated with the antidote found in the Word of God. Life can throw various curveballs at you and your swings at them may come minus a decent hit. You strike out only when you quit the ballgame. Having said that about discouragement I trust you will understand that the first step the enemy takes is to get you discouraged about a particular situation or life for that matter. This period of discouragement will soon be followed by depression, which will lead to various physical illnesses. If these are not identified and dealt with (closed) in a timely manner, the eventuality of that person is death! Did you notice that even though his ultimate purpose is death, he does not present that upfront? The people involved with marketing would refer to this as bait and switch. What appears as a "normal" problem on the surface is really deeply rooted in the bosom of evil.

Additionally, it is equally important that I point out to you there are certain things we ignorantly call bad habits, but in actuality they are "door keepers." What is a door-keeper? In this context I would like for you to understand that a doorkeeper is a spirit that comes into your life only to open the way for stronger ones to enter. For example, a person who becomes addicted to pornography did not begin with the intention that he or she would struggle with this. It is safe to say that chances are this stronghold was welcomed through the door of lust. The arrival of lust was only the starting point for a stronger spirit to make its way.

I have met countless amounts of people who are struggling with issues that modern day psychology would label as "behavioral disorders." The one lingering questions this diagnose poses for the believer is, did God create His children with behavioral disorders? If the answer is no, then from where do they find their roots? Further, notice they are labeled as disorders. This means something that what was meant to be in place, "order" is now out of order. This where is my epic struggle with the quick and uninvestigated psychological edicts finds its greatest stress. If we confine ourselves to the limited truth of these shallow versions of man's reality, we will lose sight of the more definitive nature of spiritual warfare. In the past, I would have blindly accepted and submitted to such rhetoric. However, as you navigate through Scripture, you will soon realize that the enemy will use any weapon to bring destruction to a Christian's life.

Clarice is a devoted Christian woman whose entire life has been spent in the church. She was born into a Christian family and her allegiance was directed toward the Lord Jesus Christ at a very early age. However, as she grew older, she started to struggle with certain things that were not considered proper subjects of conversation in her culture. For years she suppressed these private issues until they became masters over her young and fragile life. While actively singing in the praise and worship team, she was fighting what she later came to know as the spirit of pornography. This spirit facilitated its way through the constant viewing of adult magazines and the enjoyment of sexually explicit videos. She admitted to being addicted to anything that had a hint of pornography. For years she struggled to walk past a magazine stand that catered to her weakness. She successfully fooled everyone behind a fabricated mask of shyness and isolation.

Soon the spirit opened the door for an insatiable appetite for various men through immoral living. The weight of such oppression pushed Clarice into the arms of various men and eventually to a dual lifestyle. Her inability to exercise self-control ushered her into a whirlwind of unending confusion. When people saw her living such a promiscuous life, they often falsely condemned her without understanding that she is only catering to the resident evil spirits. How many people are in our churches like this precious lady? The convenient term to attribute is that they are carnal Christians. This is true in part, but there is a bigger problem beneath the surface. What is not seen is the slow and meticulous activities of the enemy.

Through an unparallel obedience to the Word of God, submission to the leading of the Holy Spirit and a desperate will, Clarice eventually experienced complete deliverance. Today, she is free from her bondage and her life is a testimony to the saving power of Jesus Christ. Does this story sound new to you? Well, it's not that new. Remember the Samaritan woman who encountered Jesus at the well? She too was running from a series of broken relationships. What other reason would allow her soul to be shared with six different men? What is it that drove her beyond the confines of a monogamous relationship? Who was the driving force behind her continuous starting and carelessly ending of her multiple relationships? We know it had to be none other than the author of destruction Satan himself. In addition to receiving salvation, this woman needed to be delivered from something that was stronger than she was. Though Scripture does not lay it out in detail for us, there is little doubt that many spirits including lust and greed possessed her.

Before we move further on our journey together, I wish you would allow your attention to gravitate toward Ephesians 6:12 for a moment. The passage explains that we are fighting against principalities, rulers, princes, and spirits. A close analysis of the text would confirm that there is a hierarchy within the kingdom of our adversary. In this structure, let's consider the spirits as hired or engaged runners. Their only job is to enter a life and remain anonymous forever. They are commissioned to do the work of their master. The difficulties in characterizing the enemy are truly a task that cannot be completed outside the realm of the Holy Spirit.

> Characterizing the enemy is truly a task that cannot be completed outside the realm of the Holy Spirit.

As you read this, take a moment to examine the open areas in your life that may facilitate an easy point of entry for the enemy. These doors can be opened in many ways. One of the most common ways this happens is through what we verbalize. The Book of Proverbs reminds us, "The tongue has the power of life and death" (Prov. 18:21, NIV). Another example of a way we unknowingly open doors is through the mind. A person who consistently dwells on negative things is extending an open invitation to destructive patterns and behaviors. For this reason the apostle Paul wrote to the Christians in Rome these powerful and life guiding words, "Do not conform any longer to this world, but be transformed by the renewing of your mind. Then you will be able to test and approve what God's will is—his good, pleasing and perfect will" (Rom. 12:2, NIV).

Finally, doors can be opened through the people in whose company you dwell. Relationships produce either positive or negative soul ties. The ungodly soul ties usually create openings through which the enemy can operate.

Finally, I want to remind you that in His unfailing love and grace, God has fully equipped each believer with the spirit of discernment and the necessary weapons to fight and discover their power in Him. Your deliverance is a bilateral function requiring your decisions to intersect with God's will. Closing those open doors is an indication that you are in fact opening your life to the power and presence of God.

> Your deliverance is a bilateral function requiring your decisions to intersect with God's will.

Principle 6

AUTHORITY OVER YOUR FINANCES

The rich rules over the poor,
and the borrower becomes the lender's slave.

—PROVERBS 22:7

I F I CONDUCTED a survey or gathered some people in a focus group, a major percentage of participants would agree that we live in an instant gratification society. The people on Madison Avenue have done a masterful job at creating the "If you like it, buy it" mentality. This has driven consumers to the abyss of personal debt and frustration. Have you noticed more and more retailers are offering you the buy now-pay later option? There are even special programs created for people with bad credit. Why? They have been watching as nice God-fearing people feed their need for more stuff by spending money they don't have or won't have if the behavior doesn't change.

Derrick would like for others to consider him a man of great taste. For this reason Derrick's first stop after each pay period is at the mall for a mini-shopping excursion. If asked, he will tell you that this is how he makes himself happy. His wallet is packed with every credit card one can possibly think of. He is forty-five thousand dollars deep in credit card debt and he is only adding to it. Derrick is a believer and really loves the Lord. His only time to be a part of the body is a two-hour slot on Sunday morning and then he's off to work at one of the three jobs he currently holds. A member of the care team approached him about his spending habits after the Christian counselor he was seeing gave a report about him. Derrick admitted that he had lost control of his self-esteem and his finances. The only way he knows to be accepted is to draw attention with the ongoing quest to see what new thread he is wearing. Through a series of counseling sessions and "plastic surgery" on his wallet, Derrick is on the road to recovery and health. How many people never get this chance to redeem themselves from such a financial pit?

Not having authority over your finances leads to many paralyzing events in your life. These find their culmination in the grip of the spirit of poverty. The lack of authority over ones finances leads to many ungodly dysfunctions. First of all, it robs you of the peace of mind that God desires for you. Second, it reduces precious time you could be spending with those you love and care about. The average person in America is working between fifty and seventy hours per week just to make ends meet! Who is with the kids? Unfortunately we hand them over to *Sponge Bob Square Pants* or *Dora the Explorer*; who knows what other stuff they learn from their surrogate parents, the television. Unnecessary debt forces you to work unnecessarily! God did not create us to become slaves to our pleasures. His intention is for us to live for His glory by making wise choices with the money entrusted to us. Second, a lack of authority over your finances leads to a spirit of disobedience in giving back to God. Satan usually finds a way to show us how much we can't afford to give to the work of God because of the little we have.

> Unnecessary debt forces you to work unnecessarily! God did not create us to become slaves to our pleasures.

The direct result of not handling money God's way is not having enough to tithe and invest in kingdom growth. Consequently, you can't enjoy the abundance of God's blessings and or you are extremely limited in your ability to receive them because you are not a sower. The by-product of not having enough of God's blessings in your life is to develop a spirit of envy. This is the easiest way for the enemy to rob you of your ability to live in harmony with your fellow brothers. This brings all sorts of unwanted problems into good relationships.

The basic idea here is to watch how you handle your finances because it leads to more than just being broke; it leads to being vulnerable, frustrated, and lonely! Third, lack of authority in this area eventually leads to personal destruction. Time and time again, the enemy has used financial struggle to lead to countless breakups of families and the eventual loss of future generations. Experts agree that in addition to irreconcilable differences, one of the leading causes of divorce is money. Satan uses the compulsive nature that many people in our country possess to create havoc that extends far beyond the monthly bank statement.

Robert and Sarah came to church everyday and everything seemed to be going well for this young couple and their two children. When Sarah approached me and asked me for a meeting, I thought it was to share how great things were going and how their needs were being met through the various ministries they were involved in at the church. As we got ourselves comfortable in the booth at one of my favorite restaurants, Robert began their story by explaining how the Lord had been convicting him during the current series on biblical stewardship. He openly confessed that he had lost all control over the handling of the family's finances and this was eating away at the core of their marriage. The kids were often the victims of his frustration and Sarah basically was non-existent because of the mounting bills and scarceness of funds. He explained how his affection for his family was waning due to the pressure from creditors and the guilt and shame. Sarah felt relieved that Robert was willing to take ownership for what she thought was her lack of participation in the family finances. She had begun to imagine the whole process of divorce and living as a single parent. However, Satan experienced great defeat as the Lord granted an abundance of wisdom to assist this couple with biblical guidelines regarding their finances. Today, this couple stands as a model of what God can do when you decide to take authority over the resources He has entrusted to you, especially money.

The sad reality is that we live in a society today where many people are duped by the Satan in their finances and consequently are developing unhealthy coping mechanisms. Some turn to drugs or alcohol, while others choose to lie, cheat, and steal. Moreover, there are those whom the enemy has caused to experience severe depression and others have resorted to his only offer by ending their own lives. My personal and pastoral experience has led me to identify the following steps towards gaining authority over finances.

ACTION ITEMS

1. Honor God with all you have:
   - *Biblical truth* "Honor the LORD from your wealth, and from the first of all your produce; So your barns will be filled with plenty, and your vats will overflow with new wine" (Prov. 3:9–10).

2. Plan wisely:
   - *Biblical truth* "Suppose one of you wants to build a tower. Will he not first sit down and estimate the cost to see if he has enough money to complete it?" (Luke 14:28, NIV).

3. Invest in others:

- *Biblical truth* "A generous man will prosper; he who refreshes others will himself be refreshed" (Prov. 11:25, NIV).

4. Develop the spirit of a sower:
   - *Biblical truth* "Whoever sows sparingly will also reap sparingly, and whoever sows generously will also reap generously" (2 Cor. 9:6, NIV).

STEPS FOR TODAY

1. Decide to open a savings and an IRA account.

2. Start paying your tithes this week.

STUDY QUESTIONS

1. Am I convinced that God blesses generosity?

2. In what ways have I been misusing God's financial resources? What am I willing to do to begin honoring God?

3. In what ways do you feel blessed when you act in accordance to God's Word?

Principle 7

THE BATTLEGROUND

*We demolish arguments and every pretension that sets
itself up against the knowledge of God, and we take
captive every thought to make it obedient to Christ.*

—2 Corinthians 10:5, niv

THE GREATEST BATTLE ever known to mankind
began in the Garden of Eden but has never ended.
This battle is one that is fought every second, minute
and hour of everyday. It is an epic battle for the mind of the
believer. The main ammunition is our thoughts. In every
believer's mind, there are two voices feeding information. There is the voice of God reminding you through the
Holy Spirit how precious you are in His eyes. The Spirit is
constantly announcing our freedom from sin through the
shedding of Jesus' blood. He is gently affirming us that we
are heirs of God and co-heirs of Christ. (See Romans 8:16–
17.) The Holy Spirit urges us in the direction of holiness
and total dedication to God. He comes alongside and leads

us besides still waters and restores our soul. He mends our heart through the ministry of reconciliation and redirects our focus to the Author and Finisher of our faith.

On the other hand, there is the voice of the adversary whispering our brokenness over and over again. He persists in informing us that we can never meet the standards of such a holy God. The voice reminds us of our past transgressions and our fallen humanity. Over and over again, he attempts to lead us in the path of unrighteousness through acts of disobedience and rebellion. The enemy pursues our allegiance to him and his lies with a passion that is decisive and unmatched. He takes us to the mountaintop of self-sufficiency and feeds our need to be relevant. We often can't use our God-given authority when we allow this voice to triumph over the truth of God's Word. Countless people accept a false reality from the hand of the evil one. Their acceptance of his schemes leads to a weakened faith in the sovereignty of God. The result of this is a return to ways and behaviors that eventually leads to self-destruction and painful regrets.

Joshua was a young emerging leader who showed great enthusiasm and determination. He worked tirelessly at completing his education and exercised great caution in who he allowed to enter his private world. One day while exchanging thoughts over the attributes and character of God, he made a comment that immediately raised my antenna. Joshua was struggling with accepting the fact that God does love him and wants to have a relationship with him. You see, he was rejected by his father from the earliest age he could recall. His father's words were always piercing as he reminded him over and over again of how he would never amount to anything and that his final home would be a prison cell until he died. To cope with such a rough and unstable foundation, Joshua developed a great façade carefully covered by the veneer of busyness. He hid behind the many talents and abilities God gave him. Joshua and I began an unforced relationship that eventually led to a time of discipleship. Using Scripture and real life examples of people who had successfully overcome similar beginnings, we began to confess what the Word of God says. This led Joshua to begin accepting a truth that he had questioned for most of his life. Today, he is doing well and has a healthy outlook on life. He is passionate about God and his zeal for ministry is uncommon. What happened? God invaded Joshua's mind with the real truth—His Word.

Remember the words of Jesus. He has given us authority over all the powers of enemy and nothing will serve as a hindrance for us. In order for this to be manifested in our lives, we must yield to the truth of God's inerrant Word and allow our minds to be transformed by His Spirit. Remember this truth: your mind is God's gift to you, and how you use it is your gift to Him. It is safe to say that our mind is the battlefield on which the enemy rages war with our destiny.

> Your mind is God's gift to you, and how you use it is your gift to Him.

ACTION ITEMS

1. Renew your mind daily:
   - *Biblical truth* "And do not be conformed to this world, but be transformed by the renewing of your mind, that you may prove what the will of God is, that which is good and acceptable and perfect" (Rom. 12:2).

2. Recognize your spiritual position in Christ:
   - *Biblical truth* "For you have not received a spirit of slavery leading to fear again, but you have received a spirit of adoption as sons by which we cry out 'Abba! Father!' The Spirit Himself bears witness with our spirit that we are children of God, and if children, heirs also, heirs of God and fellow heirs with Christ" (Rom. 8:15–17).

3. Set your mind upwards:
   - *Biblical truth* "If then you have been raised up with Christ, keep seeking the things above, where Christ is, seated at the right hand of God. Set your mind on the things above, not on the things that are on earth" (Col. 3:1–2).

STEPS FOR TODAY

1. Renew your mind by repeating that you are child of God redeemed by the blood of Jesus.

2. Challenge the thoughts that come to you throughout the day.

STUDY QUESTIONS

1. What issues am I always thinking about?

2. How much of my attention is focused on the Holy Spirit throughout the day?

3. Where do I experience tension with my thoughts?

Principle 8

AUTHORITY OVER SELF

For the good that I wish, I do not do; but I practice the very evil that I do not wish.... Wretched man that I am! Who will set me free from the body of this death?

—ROMANS 7:19, 24

HAVE YOU EVER set out on a trip with a delightful destination only to incur delay after delay? Better yet, have you ever timed a well-known route only to encounter an unexpected detour? The frustration that comes with this experience at times tests our patience and determination. Our humanity, better known as the flesh, often gets in the way of the Spirit's direction. When this occurs, we often find ourselves running up against the will and purposes of God for our lives. This is the torment Paul found himself in when he mercifully asked, "Who will set me free from the body of this death?"

Like Paul every believer is trapped in the grip of two natures. There is the one that desires to honor God and then there is the one that seeks its own fulfillment and gratification through whichever means necessary. The responsibility of the Christian is to make every effort to live a life that is totally surrendered to God. As Paul wrote to the Galatians, this is not easily done. Authority over self requires the acceptance of another nature to have preeminence. That nature is the one birthed by the Holy Spirit at the point of acceptance and is developed over a lifetime through a process known as sanctification. This occurs when we come to the end of ourselves and we ask God to reign over every area of our lives. In addition, the transforming work of the cross must be valued and accepted as our currency towards the righteousness that God demands. To simply put it, the believer's authority over self happens when he or she arrives at a complete understanding that Christ has the right to rule over their life. Paul confessed this when he noted his ability to accept where he was in life. He said, "I can do all things through Him who strengthens me" (Phil. 4:13).

> The responsibility of the Christian is to make every effort to live a life that is totally surrendered to God.

ACTION ITEMS

1. Commit to less of you:
   - *Biblical truth* "He must increase, but I must decrease" (John 3:30).

2. Practice righteousness:
   - *Biblical truth* "But seek first His kingdom and His righteousness; and all these things shall be added to you" (Matt. 6:33).

3. Exercise the fruit of the Spirit:
   - *Biblical truth* "But the fruit of the Spirit is love, joy, peace, patience, kindness, goodness, faithfulness, gentleness, and self-control" (Gal. 5:22).

STEPS FOR TODAY

1. Revisit your current life goals.

2. Practice patience as you drive today.

STUDY QUESTIONS

1. When was the last time you lost your temper?

2. What insight has God given you concerning exercising self-control?

3. What might cause you to lose your focus on holiness?

Principle 9

AUTHORITY OF THE SPOKEN WORD

The tongue has the power of life and death.
—**PROVERBS 18:21, NIV**

J ANE WALKED INTO my office with a face that appeared worn and totally discouraged. As she sat down she quickly let out a scream, "I can't take it anymore!" "What is it?" I asked, in the midst of my shock. With tears welling up in her eyes, she looked at me and said, "The constant verbal abuse, Pastor, the beating up from his mouth." While she did not appear visibly damaged from any physical abuse, she looked downtrodden from something that hurts more than a punch or a shove. The words hurled at her by the person who promised to love her until death brought separation, was now killing her will to live and fight through adversity. I use this real-life example to illustrate how powerful the spoken word can be over someone's life. Words are not as innocent as we tend to think they are. Words carry meaning and that meaning is a part of our reality.

> **Words carry meaning and that meaning is a part of our reality.**

As a believer, you ought to understand that when you confess the written Word, you are speaking life over situations the flesh cannot fight on its own. The weapon of open confession is one of the most potent components of your artillery. The enemy does not like to hear the quoted Word of God. Indeed, there is life and death in words and you should understand what you are saying and why you're saying it. Many Christians live defeated lives because they don't understand this particular dimension of authority as given by Christ. The lack of understanding leads them to label this as a "name it and claim it" movement. Far be it from that! Confessing the Word of God over your life demonstrates your understanding of who God is in His fullness and knowing who you are through Jesus Christ. The Bible says you have not because you ask not. (See James 4:2.) My friend it doesn't get any simpler than that. Your confession determines your possession. I often tell the people when I preach that there are two things you can do when situations arise in your life. First, you can speak to it, or you can speak against it. Know that your words order your world.

> **Your confession determines your possession.**

Allow me to borrow your sense of logic for a moment. When the doctor comes out of the room with the report that reveals a spot on the liver or a lump in the right breast, your natural reaction is fear of the unknown. Your next step can lead to ruin or resolve. There is no doubt that, your human reaction of fear and hopelessness is a direct result of a "supposed truth" that has just been confessed. At first you believe it because this is a professional who would not play games with your emotions. Why on earth then is it so difficult to believe the God who is the creator of the universe and the giver of life? God's written Word is the compass that guides when the ship is threatened by rough waves and perilous conditions. His Word is the platform from which we announce our confidence and victory over the enemy. Words are the guardian of our destiny. Any parent knows this very well. If you speak into the life of child things that are not positive, you can bet the return on that investment will be an individual who produces behaviors that are distasteful to society.

> God's written Word is the compass that guides when the ship is threatened by rough waves and perilous conditions. Words are the guardian of our destiny.

There was a mother who prayed endlessly for the future of her only son. She carried his picture in her Bible and requested the intercession of other saints for this wayward child. Ronald was living under a series of ungodly confessions made over his life by his father who was a deacon in the church! His father took every opportunity to inform him of how his life would have no relevance in society because he was not serious enough in his pursuit of a promising future. The father made his jovial personality the subject of many tirades. He lived in a mental deficit created by his immediate surroundings. He was constantly being compared to the son of another deacon. At the age of eighteen, like any other teenager living under such a dark and guilt ridden paternalistic spell, Ronald gave up on church and any fragile faith he had in God. He began living the life of a vagabond and was bringing grief to his mother's heart. Each time the phone rang, she expected the call that would let her know that her son's miserable life had come to an end. I spoke to Ronald and asked him why he chose to live this lifestyle. He explained to me that he was never given a chance to escape the mouth of his father. Words are not just words; they carry power!

You can agree with me that words do carry meaning, right? If this is true and we acknowledge it when we see people reacting to the way they were spoken to growing up; then it is only fair that we admit that by speaking God's Word, we have His divine favor to walk in victory.

I met a young lady during a recent trip to a city I will leave unidentified. She occupied the same seat each night as I shared the message for this annual conference. Before the closing service, she slipped me a piece of paper requesting that I give her fifteen minutes of my time before leaving that evening. With much reservation, I agreed to listen to her. She began by thanking me for the way God used me to speak truth into her life with each message she heard.

However, she went on to tell me how much she hated living and that she was seriously weighing the option of shortening her earthly experience. As the conversation progressed, I probed a little deeper to unveil the cause of her distorted view of the life God had given her. She confessed to me that her past has become a shadow and it covers anything she is attempting to accomplish. She feels worthless and unwanted by society because her testimony is not so perfect before the people of the church. The most unbelievable thing is that she also believes that her story is not one that God may have allowed her to experience. At that moment, the Holy Spirit led me to ask her one questions, and it went like this "Who told you what you have believed"? At that moment silence ruled the entire room. At issue here was a disconnect between the reality of God's transforming power and the shame of her past.

As a child of God adopted into His family through Jesus Christ, you must begin to confess that you are blessed and not cursed; you are the highly favored seed of Abraham. You must declare that you are forgiven and no longer a slave to sin. You are the righteousness of God and you have been justified by the shed blood of Christ. Moreover, He has traded your sorrows for joy and has turned your mourning into dancing. Additionally, you must declare that because of the peace that surpasses all understanding, you are not anxious about anything. These are not positive thoughts designed to make you feel good, but these are life confessions you need to speak when the adversary comes to remind you of your old nature. It is at this point you engage the life-changing words of the apostle Paul, "Therefore if any man is in Christ, he is a new creature; the old things passed away; behold, new things have come" (2 Cor. 5:17). Paul wrote to the Christians living in Rome these words to remind them that they are no longer victims but victors, "Therefore, there is now no condemnation for those who are in Christ Jesus, because through Christ Jesus the law of the Spirit of life set me free from the law of sin and death" (Rom. 8:1–2, NIV). Speak as one who is free and confess that freedom in the face of life's attempts to keep you in bondage.

ACTION ITEMS

1. Study the Word of God:
   - *Biblical truth* "Be diligent to present yourself approved to God as workman who does not need to be ashamed, handling accurately the word of truth" (2 Tim. 2:15).

2. Confess the Word through faith:
   - *Biblical truth* "If you have faith as small as a mustard seed, you can say to this mountain, 'Move from here to there' and it will move. Nothing will be impossible for you" (Matt. 17:20, NIV).

3. Use the sword:
   - *Biblical insight* "For the word of God is living and active. Sharper than any double-edged

sword, it penetrates even to dividing soul and spirit, joints and marrow" (Heb. 4:12, NIV).

STEPS FOR TODAY

1. Commit to reading an entire Psalm before the end of the day.

2. Reverse every negative thought into a godly thought.

STUDY QUESTIONS

1. In what ways do you feel challenged in your knowledge of God's Word?

2. What new insights do you have about the power of the Word in the believer's life?

3. Can you recall an instance where the Word came through for you?

Principle 10

AUTHORITY OVER
YOUR INTENTIONS

Search me, O God, and know my heart;
try me and know my anxious thoughts.

—Psalm 139:23

AMONG GOD'S GREATEST gifts to humanity, the power of intention must be prominently placed the top of that list. Theologically we may refer to this as your will, but for the sake of this lesson let's stick with the term intention. Your life now is the sum total of your choices in the past. Your choices are an observable reflection of your hidden or unspoken intention. Every action taken by someone is driven by a motive for good or evil. Take for example someone who loves to eat rum raisin ice cream. Each time they purchase a cone or a pint of it, their main objective is to satisfy the pleasure they get from eating that particular treat. In the same manner, each behavior a person engages in, is birthed in the bosom of intention.

> Your choices are an observable reflection of your hidden or unspoken intention.

We often trivialize sin by not taking ownership of the reality of intention. It is so easy to conveniently transfer the responsibility for our personal choices to another person, our parents, the community into which we were born, or even the government. This selective ignorance often results in a colossal failure to really understand how effective the enemy's schemes can be.

> We often trivialize sin by not taking ownership of the reality of intention.

People do the things they deem important and fulfilling. A person who resorts to a bottle of whiskey when life gets hard is doing so with the intention of forgetting the reality he is living in. The woman who seeks love in needless relationships fools herself by thinking she is moving towards her intended destination of love and contentment. The young man who is now dying with AIDS because he looked for himself in other men did so with the intention of finding love and affection. That son who now sits in a prison cell with a life sentence for gang-related activities is there because the need for affection and acceptance was his intention when he agreed to become a part of the group. Can you see where I am going with this? Intentions are missiles that propel us either to our place of rest and contentment—or total depravation.

> Intentions are missiles that propel
> us either to our place of rest and
> contentment—or total depravation.

The fall greatly affected our intentions as we slipped into a broken humanity never intended by God. A closer look at the story of humanity in Scripture reveals a steady decline in "well intentioned" behavior. From the murder of Abel by his brother Cain, to the outright rebellion of Jonah, man has always looked for ways to do what seems good to him. However, God is calling us to allow Him to direct our intentions. The invitation is for complete surrender of yourself under the mighty hand of God. The apostle Paul illustrated this for us in his declaration of turmoil. He states, "The things I should do, I don't, and the things I should not do, I do." (See Romans 7:14–15.) My friend, that is one of the purest examples of an honest struggle with intention. The intentional act of allowing God's Spirit to direct your existence moves you closer to the high calling that God has placed on your life. Once you begin to understand the position you hold as a child of God, it is easier for you to begin exercising authority over your intentions.

ACTION ITEMS

1. Learn to die:
   - *Biblical truth* "I have been crucified with Christ; and it is no longer I who live, but Christ lives in me; and the life which I now live in the flesh I live by faith in the Son of God" (Gal. 2:20).

2. Become an authentic servant:
   - *Biblical truth* "For even the Son of Man did not come to be served, but to serve, and to give His life a ransom for many" (Mark 10:45).

3. Commit to doing good:
   - *Biblical truth* "Do not withhold good from those who deserve it, when it is in your power to act" (Prov. 3:27, NIV).

STEPS FOR TODAY

1. Serve someone with no expected return.

2. Intentionally bless someone with a gift card.

STUDY QUESTIONS

1. Explain what it means to surrender. Have you completely surrendered your will to Christ?

2. What new insight has God given to you about your intentions?

3. How does it feel to have control over your intentions?

Principle 11

AUTHORITY OVER YOUR PAST

Therefore if any man is in Christ,
he is a new creature;
the old things passed away;
behold, new things have come.

—2 CORINTHIANS 5:17

ER FACE LIT up when we concluded the final weeks of an intensive twelve-week counseling session. After each session I watched as the bounce came back into her step; she was set free. The balance on her bank statement had not changed that much, but she had finally understood and renounced the spirits that had pursued her for over twenty years. She was free from her past and looking towards a future with promise for the first time.

The enemy understands the power of the past, and he constantly seeks to use that against you as a child of God. I am not just talking of your educational history or your career, I am talking about past actions and decisions that have been hijacked by an evil spirit and is now attempting to wreak havoc over your life and future. As the gracious father He is, God reminds us that He does not remember our sins anymore. In the Bible we read, "I, even I, am the one who wipes out your transgressions for My own sake; and I will not remember your sins" (Isa. 43:25). You need to understand and accept that your past is exactly that—your past. That is not who you are today because the blood of Jesus has placed you under a new covenant.

Geri was adamant about her decision to never enter the institution of marriage because of the hurt inflicted by several ungodly men, some who were married themselves. Her disdain for men was the foundation of her resentment and anger. She rebelled against any authority that represented itself in a male form. She recalls how many traffic citations could have been avoided only if the patrol officer was of the opposite sex. Her past of being physically abused placed a cloud over her ability to differentiate between yesterday and today. She preferred to go from one relationship to another and shun anyone of them she thought had the hint of becoming serious. Why? Her past spoke loudly and was now drowning her ability to hear the voice of God calling her His child. Unfortunately, Geri is not alone in this particular world.

Taking authority over your past begins in your mind. There are various streams of thoughts and deceptions coming at you everyday. You can make the choice to believe what the enemy is throwing at you or you can decide that you are who God says you are. New fruits need new roots. To stop eating the spoiled fruits of the past, you must engage in planting new roots. The roots I am arguing for here are the ones that can only be found in your new identity. The apostle Paul helps us understand this recreated identity this way. This born-again apostle of Jesus Christ writes, "The Spirit Himself bears witness with our spirit that we are children of God, and if children, heirs also, heirs of God and fellow heirs with Christ" (Rom. 8:16–17). That truth is worth resting on for the rest of your life on this earth! The enemy tries to defeat that by getting you to trade your spiritual position in Christ with a spirit of guilt and shame.

New fruits need new roots.

You are not who you thought you were. God did not create you as damaged goods. His Word teaches us that he has crowned us with Glory. I am still trying to comprehend the depth of what the writer of Psalm 8 meant when he wrote these life-giving words, "What is man, that Thou dost take thought of him? And the son of man, that Thou dost care for him? Yet Thou hast made him a little lower than God, and dost crown him with glory and majesty!" (Ps. 8:4–5). Shout amen!

ACTION ITEMS

1. Know your identity:
   - *Biblical truth* "And God created man in His own image, in the image of God He created him; male and female He created them" (Gen. 1:27).

2. Allow the past to come to an end:
   - *Biblical truth* "Do not call to mind the former things, or ponder things of the past. Behold, I will do something new, now it will spring forth; Will you not be aware of it? I will even make a roadway in the wilderness, rivers in the desert" (Isa. 43:18–19).

3. Look ahead with purpose:
   - *Biblical truth* "One thing I do: forgetting what lies behind and reaching forward to what lies ahead, I press on toward the goal for the prize of the upward call of God in Christ Jesus" (Phil. 3:13–14, NIV).

STEPS FOR TODAY

1. Rebuke the guilty feeling for the things that happened before you read this book.

2. Write down five positive things you hope to accomplish in the next six months.

STUDY QUESTIONS

1. In what ways are you feeling challenge by your past?

2. What new insight has God given you about His role in erasing your past?

3. Can you remember a time when your past prevented you from moving onto God's agenda?

Principle 12

AUTHORITY OVER YOUR FREEDOM

Act as free men, do not use your freedom as covering for evil, but use it as bondslaves of God.

—1 PETER 2:16

I HAVE SPENT THE first eleven chapters attempting to outline specific areas of your life that you need to gain control of through the divine authority God has given you. Now I want to ask you to practice these by exercising authority over your newfound freedom. Better yet, it's not newly found as much as it is revelation given to you by the Spirit through this book.

I have already identified several ways for you to gain true freedom from the grip of demonic activities over your life. These timeless, biblical truths are particularly critical as you advance towards a Spirit-filled life. When we combine the insights concerning the power of God and His power in the life of each believer, we can then understand why it is absolutely necessary to exercise authority over our newly discovered or better yet, rediscovered freedom.

Freedom is not freedom without responsibility! Let me give you a simple example. Those of us who call America home are very fortunate for the freedom we enjoy. You may think that it's hard to live in this country; however, your opinion quickly changes whenever you travel to places where fear, political oppression, economic distress, poverty, sickness and intimidation are the order of the day.

> Freedom is not freedom without responsibility!

I had the privilege of traveling to Asia recently and my love for the United States grew with each hour I was there. The spiritual oppression mixed with an unbalanced level of poverty forced me to question what is it that we have the right to complain about? The people were not free to practice their faith if it was not the faith endorsed by the state. One church planter shared with me an interesting story of how he was almost beheaded in a village for sharing Christ. What struck me was his resolve to share about his freedom in Christ, in spite of persecution. He understood that with spiritual freedom comes responsibility.

Let me say it clearly—it is a blessing to live in America! However, with all the freedom and our unalienable rights that are guaranteed by the Constitution, as citizens we have an obligation to practice responsibility. Why? When we fail to do so, we infringe upon someone else's freedom.

Have you ever noticed that every miracle Jesus performed

included two things: freedom and responsibility. At the pool of Bethesda, Jesus healed a man who had been lame for the better part of thirty-eight years. After receiving the freedom of his legs again, Jesus meets him at the temple and cautions him with these words, "Behold, you have become well; do not sin anymore, so that nothing worse may befall you" (John 5:14). His encounter with the woman caught in adultery by the Pharisees included an undeserved pardon and freedom from death by stones. More importantly, it also included a responsibility to go and sin no more. Jesus gave Zaccheus the chance of a lifetime. However, he was to discontinue robbing people as a tax collector. Some of you are probably wishing Jesus could come and have a conversation like that with your local tax collector's office. It isn't going to happen!

It is safe to say that salvation is freedom. Knowing Jesus and accepting His sacrificial work on the cross has to be the greatest truth in the world. However, Paul warns us not to take that freedom for granted. He writes to the believers at Philippi in this manner, "So then, my beloved, just as you have always obeyed, not as in my presence only, but now much more in my absence, work out your salvation with fear and trembling" (Phil. 2:12). Before you Biblical scholars get all bent out of shape on the proper rules of hermeneutics, the idea I am trying to convey is that our Spirit of freedom in Christ must be accompanied by a holy fear and reverence for God.

> Our Spirit of freedom in Christ must be accompanied by a holy fear and reverence for God.

ACTION ITEMS

1. Appreciate the price of freedom:
   - *Biblical truth* "It was for freedom that Christ set us free; therefore keep standing firm and do not be subject again to a yoke of slavery" (Gal. 5:1).

2. Accept truth and live free:
   - *Biblical truth* "And you shall know the truth, and the truth shall make you free" (John 8:32, NIV).

3. Represent freedom:
   - *Biblical truth* "I, therefore, the prisoner of the Lord, entreat you to walk in a manner worthy of the calling with which you have been called" (Eph. 4:1, NIV).

STEPS FOR TODAY

1. Confess your freedom in Christ continually.

2. Identify one thing that you have no control over and ask God to deliver you from it.

STUDY QUESTIONS

1. Can you recall a time when your freedom was a source of pain for someone else?

2. What new insight has God given you about freedom and responsibility?

3. What is your definition of Christian liberty?

CLOSING THOUGHTS

AS I WRITE the closing lines of this book, I am clueless as to how you will apply these timeless principles in your life. I've seen amazing things happen in people who "claim" to get this. God's Spirit is at work in bringing truth to the lives of His people. Further, the Holy Spirit is at work in the ways we are learning the vices of the enemy. It is also at work in bringing healing, purpose, freedom, and deliverance to those seeking it. In this light it becomes abundantly clear that Christians are more than just a group of co-dependant fanatics. We are, in fact, in a cooperative work with the triune God in demonstrating the undeniable victory we have over Satan and his powerless kingdom.

The argument of the previous pages shows how God has a way of bringing revolution to places where resignation once settled in. I can only speak of the personal transformation that has occurred in my family and ministry because of my understanding that God has granted me authority in everyday life. If you dare join me in exploring the power that God has invested in each of you, it is guaranteed that your life will never be the same. The enemy has no power over you except the power you give him. Begin your journey towards true freedom today and experience an overflow of God's richest provisions for you. Remember this, you have no control over what took place in your life yesterday, but with God on your side, you can determine your tomorrow and the future seasons. You are on the cusp of something greater than your past or present circumstance. Go ahead, grab a hold of it and don't let it slip away this time, because now you have the authority to get it, keep it, and live it!

LET'S PRAY AS YOU EMBARK ON THIS LIFE-CHANGING JOURNEY

I now cancel and revoke every agreement I made with Satan and his schemes by commission or omission. I completely renounce any voluntary ties and I re-possess my heart, will, and mind in the name of Jesus. Standing on the Word of God and through the power of Jesus I bind him and command him to flee.

MY PRAYERFUL WISH FOR YOU

I pray that the eyes of your heart may be enlightened, so that you may know what is the hope of His calling, what are the riches of the glory of His inheritance in the saints.

—Ephesians 1:18